LIGHT and AFTER
Kobus Moolman

DEEP SOUTH

ISBN: 978-0-9584915-7-0

Deep South
PO Box 6082
Grahamstown
6140
South Africa

Deep South titles are distributed by
University of KwaZulu-Natal Press
www.ukznpress.co.za

Edited by: Robert Berold
Layout and design: Katie Wilter
Cover painting: Kokerboom Koppie by Lyn Gilbert

for Julia

soli deo gloria

by Kobus Moolman

Poetry
Separating the Seas
Feet of the Sky
5 Poetry (contributor)
Time like Stone
Anatomy (limited edition chapbook illustrated by Witty Nyide)

Drama
Full Circle
Blind Voices: a collection of radio plays

Editor
Tilling the Hard Soil: Poetry and Prose
by South African Writers with Disabilities

Now the wind sends its rails ahead;
we will follow in slow trains
and inhabit these islands,
trust beside trust.

- Ingeborg Bachmann

Contents

Home

Light

Anatomy

Afterwards

HOME

Moving

The house was empty. In his dream.

A modern house. Large rooms. Polished tiled floors.

The house was empty, except for a green plastic table in the dining room. The garden furniture variety. A plastic table only. No chairs.

And he was sweeping the floor. In his dream. Because there were hundreds of small dry seeds all over the floor. Small white seeds. Just like you might find in a pepper. And he was sweeping them up with a grass broom into a pile underneath the table.

From all over the house.

Sweeping. Sweeping.

And the more he swept – fetching them now from the shiny kitchen, now from the cold bedrooms – the more he found.

It was night. The doors were open. Big glass sliding doors. He could hear the crickets or the frogs in the dark garden. As he swept.

It was their new house. With all the lights on. Their shiny, new, empty house. With large rooms. And that peculiar, slightly sinister, echo that all empty houses have. Houses that have not been domesticated yet.

The untamed silence. Of the new.

And then it happened.

The electronic motor-gate suddenly opened. All on its own. Suddenly. The large metal gate just trundled back slowly on its small metal wheels. Trundled along its metal track. Open.

And slowly shut. All on its own.

And opened again. With a life of its own. Open and shut. Slowly. Open and shut. In his dream.

Because something was coming in. Which he could not see.

Something was coming in. And going out again. Coming in. And going out again. Unable to make up its mind. Something he could not see. Of unrecognisable shape. Something he sensed only. With the hairs on his skin.

The way animals sense danger.

The Solution

It came to him just as he was falling asleep. The solution to his dilemma.

Whether he should stay where he was. In the house with the crack in the floor and the lifting tiles. In the house where the doors stuck in their frames and the shelves leaned precariously.

Or whether he should scrape together all his savings and buy a boat. And sail away from the concrete and glass shore (even though he got sea-sick and couldn't swim) and disappear over the horizon.

It came to him just as he was falling asleep. The solution to the dilemma that had been pursuing him like a wild beast in his dreams and waking him up in the middle of the night, wet with sweat and shivering.

Whether he should trust the yellow clay and the black shale under his feet; sink his toes into the mud and allow them to take root and grow.

Or whether he should open his mouth and his nose and his eyes and leap into the rolling water and inhale the atmosphere of the cold waves.

Just as he felt himself slipping away from his thoughts, into a vacuum, it shook him awake. The solution.

He would buy the boat. Yes. He would sail away from the shore of steel and stone. He would risk his life on the unstable waves.

Immediately he sprang out of his small bed. He pulled on his clothes, a warm jacket for the wind and a woollen hat. Down the stairs he hastened, and flung the front door open onto the street.

The street outside his house had disappeared. It had fallen into a great crack in the earth. The crack that ran through the middle of his house. And he fell into the black vacuum. And the last thing he saw, as the black wave of the pit closed over him, was a boat, a small wooden rowing boat, sailing empty-handed into the sky.

The Door

In the night he gets up. Driven by the need to piss. Although it is dark, he can make out the faintly white expanse of the door. He does not switch on the light. The room is small. Yet it feels as if he has taken longer to get to the other side of the room than he should have. He reaches for the door handle. But it is not there. He moves his hand to the left. To the right. Up. Down. But he cannot find the handle. How can this be? This is surely the stuff of dreams. But he is awake. Of that he is certain. He sweeps his hand in large arcs across the hard surface of the door. He reaches low. He reaches high. It is impossible, he knows, for the handle to be this low. Or this high. But he must try. Again and again. With increasing perplexity. Increasing panic. What has happened in the night to the room while he was sleeping? How will he get out now? Is he trapped forever? Finally he admits that he cannot find the handle. There is nothing else for it. He must turn on the light. For a moment – a dreadful moment – he cannot find the light switch. And it flashes through his mind that he is not in his room at all. That he is somewhere else. Where no one will ever find him. But then his hand feels the cold plastic of the switch. His hand recognises the mechanism. And knows what to do. He closes his eyes just before he turns on the switch. He closes his eyes so that he will not be blinded by the sudden light. And it is then that he discovers the truth. That he has not been standing by the door at all. As he had believed. That all this time, in the darkness and in his abstraction, he had been trying to open a solid wall.

Watched

Something snaps close behind him. And he whips around.

But there is no one there.

Has he imagined the sound? There is only the wind. And the thin sunlight on all sides of him. The shrieking of beetles.

He turns back and resumes writing in his black school notebook. Writing about a man interrupted in his writing by the sound of something snapping close behind him.

It is the middle of the morning. Ants are carrying away the earth beneath his feet. The cicadas are on fire. A crow in a coroner's apron lands on a wooden fence. And watches him.

Behind him the bushes crack their long fingers.

He does not dare to move.

The shadows of the trees and the shadows of the bushes take on the shape of an intangible sky.

The Window

It is a large window without any curtains.

A large window with unpainted wooden frames. And thick black burglar guards.

A large window with a wooden door set into the middle. And a steel gate with one, two, three small padlocks. One on top, one in the middle, and the last lock at the bottom.

It is a large window. Which he will have to get to know.

It is a large window with a view onto the sun-soaked side of his garden. Which he will have to find a way to understand.

A large window that refuses to look at him.

That treats him like a non-entity.

The Room

He lies in a small room with the curtains closed.
>   In a small room with the curtains closed in the middle of
>   the day and the sun outside swinging a broad blade.

He lies in a small room on a narrow metal bed.
>   In a small room on a narrow metal bed, wearing long
>   grey trousers and a white sleeveless vest, with his black
>   shoes under the bed, on the left, and his feet, in long
>   grey socks, pointing up and slightly away from each
>   other.

He lies in a small room in the dim underwater light.
>   In a small room in the dim underwater light with his
>   arms folded and his damp white chest moving slowly up
>   and down.

He lies in a small room with his eyes closed and dreams of the
>   cloudless sky striking the stone church outside.
>   In a small room with his eyes closed and dreams of a
>   sky without any wind or moisture or wings or mobility or
>   colour or bottom.

A sky that echoes like a room after all the contents have been
>   removed, and only the dust-lines along the wall remain
>   to indicate old habits.
>   That echoes like a man on a narrow bed in a small room
>   with his eyes closed, and the whole world collapsing
>   inside his head.

Wind

A tree without leaves
wind sprouting
from its long branches

A sky without birds
wind flapping
around its wide corner

A mouth without tongue
wind stumbling
about its dark hole.

Winter Trees

Beneath the bare trees
stripped to sky, and
smelling of dust, two old
hands hold, fold and re-
fold a thin sheet of earth.
'Where is the wind? And
why is the wind never
a tree anymore?' the hands ask,
folding. 'The bare branches
of the bare trees no longer
hold anything. All falls
through the thin earth.
Why, even the sky,' the hands
say, 'has dropped all of
its clouds.'

The Mountain

At night the mountain
is a sky, cold and blank.
The mountain is the memory
of a name departed,
washed out from the loud
drum of day, day's hard
blade of blue. At night
the mountain is a silence
hunkered between
absence and feeling;
the swelling sound a
voice makes through the mist
of longing, the mist of
remembering. The mountain
is a sky, a voice climbing up
out of the black air.

Old Town

Sky closed over
grey slate cold stone
brown hills black tar
rock buried beneath

Thin light cold hands
rusted old steel trees
stiff wind small birds
exploding leaves

Hands black smoke
over old burning
birth place.

Before Dawn

Early up. Darkness
tries out a small tongue:

rooster, rock pigeon
and donkey.

Tightly packed. Sky
tries on silent shapes:

hunchbacked hill, pine
tree and shed.

Return to bed. Same old
stories to fall asleep to:

stick without foot,
twisted spine of night.

Three Trees

Three ghosts of trees
swim on a hillside
in the mist.

Left behind, the light
of the full moon
shines a faint trail.

Loud, the river repeats
a stencil of waves
across the black air.

Three ghosts of trees
wait for hanging
three old messages upon.

Loxton – Karoo – Dusk

All day the wind
has carried the light on its back
across the cracked stones.

**

The stones were born
without legs. They must use
their eyes to move.

**

The wind counts on old fingers
all the birds' wings it takes
to build a mountain.

Umfolozi

Crooked thorn tree
overlooking a green valley

Purple distance
ploughing up clods of cloud

Sky of white glass
sharpening sun's fingers

Black hawk
twisting off a thermal.

False Bay

The sea is green
the mountain black

the wind hefts iron.

We stand here on the edge
together and look

out until we cannot see –

A thick grey cloud comes
suddenly out of nowhere

slams the pathway shut.

Opening

The light is green and thin
beneath the shadow of the sky.

A rooster carries the dawn
across the sun, behind the hill.

The wind and all its leaves
are slow and water-logged.

In the hole of a man's hand
a clenched heart slowly opens.

Hunger

And God gave the man little wingless birds,
small as a shock,
to eat while He was away.

And a cup the size of a scab,
in case His return was delayed,
and the rain ran out.

But the man ate all the birds on the first day,
he was so hungry, and by
the second, the scab was picked raw.

Now the man has nothing left
to live on except
the dirt under his fingernails.

He doesn't know what he is going to do
when the third day comes
and goes without Him.

Beneath the Yellow Moon

Beneath the yellow moon
the ice in his heart
burns

Between the blades of the wind
his dripping hand
stammers

Behind the long bridge of the sky
his floating eyes splinter
in betrayal.

Winter Dawn

The sky starts last in these parts.

Unforeseen rain sinks a house
into the mud of insomnia.

Black-frost is the only sense
the bare leaves have left.

The sky has a long way
still to travel before dawn.

Theft

Stolen from a grey cloud
two breaths: one shirtless
and scratched, the other
thin as dish-water, rheumy.

Stolen from a grey sky
a bowl of soup and two
hands; one with long fingers,
the other with a ring.

Burial

Light underground hums
the iron of a tunnel

Black worm turns
blank eyes up to the dark

The sound of crumbling
keeps decomposing stones alive.

Two Moons

There are two moons
in this sky tonight, this dark
hole with no sides.

Hold onto the steep earth,
decipher the meaning of the lights
at both ends of the darkness:

One the colour of milk
with its smell, the other red
and thirsty as transfusion.

Three Views of a Pair of Orthopaedic Boots

Tired boot
twists on the
rope of the body

$$* * *$$

Dry boot
squeaks like a
rusted guillotine

$$* * *$$

Brown boot
longs to be
ash-black again.

Boy

(for Fahamu Pecou)

He looks at the world
and is frightened

by the size of what
his hands will become.

Will his dreams ever fit
into such an old space?

Already he can feel
the pinch of the sky.

Already the light is too small
for his new wings.

That Day
(for Gabi Nkosi: shot 26 May 2008)

Gun-grey day.

A big brown horse
bent at a lake.

The hills in a haze.

Slow horse surrounded
by the rowing of water.

Metal-black trees.

A cock with
a hoarse voice crowing.

Sky with a hole.

The light leaking out
all the way from beyond.

Insomnia

Once again he cannot sleep.
He lies in bed with his eyes shut and the blood
pooling in his belly.

Once again sleep eludes him like light through his fingers.

Once again he gets up, puts on his feet, pours out his eyes
into the dark lake of his window.

The window gathers silence tightly around him like a shawl.

The silence has the colour of night. The colour
of sleepless remembering.

Ambition

Yesterday he could easily still believe
that getting to the top really amounted to something.
That if he had a goal, he would ultimately reach it.

Today he woke up
and saw himself in the small mirror behind the bathroom door,
and saw the cuts under his eyes,
the holes in his hands.

And at that moment he knew
that the body is not flesh, it does not feel.
That it is made of sand instead. And it runs out.

Survival

We who accept survival as our password

accept incompleteness as our blessing.

We who dress in blindness and in faith

do not know the colour of our palms

nor the weight of our feet upon the water.

We who have dust in our mouths all day

have stones instead of songs on our tongues.

We who quench fire with fire all night

know that wings are not the only ladders

to the dark, that heavy wood swims too

in the tide of the wind.

We who accept survival

accept survival as our curse.

ANATOMY

The Hand

This is the hand. Talking.

This is me. Holding up the hand
and looking hard into it.

Is anyone listening?

The hand swims through the quick
water of daylight, through the slow
water of the night.
The hand burns during the day and
curls into brown smoke.
The hand burns at night and
crackles with electricity.
It jumps when anyone walks past.
It gasps and swallows short breaths
and stumbles over its broken teeth
when anyone asks it a question.

Is anyone listening?

I do not want to listen.
I do not want to sit and wait,
holding the hand in my hand
like a woman in the cold, a woman in the
cold and the dark cradling a dead child,
like a woman cradling nothing.

I hear the hand all day.
I hear it whispering behind walls.
Behind thin doors.
I hear it in my dreams. In my desire.

My lust is filled with the dark
blood of the hand, the dark light
that pulls, that calls, pulls
like a heavy rope at my heart.

I look at the hand and see
the scars of fires and knives.

I look at the hand and see
the calluses of stones and sticks.

I look at the hand and hear
the slow bending of bone, the curling
tongue of tissue and vein as the old words of my heart
close upon themselves like a leaf,
like the leaves of plants in dry lands
desperate to preserve the little that
remains in their veins.

I hear the hand call out, and turn my back.

I turn away from the sight of its large fingers
curled around the hole in my back,
its hard skin closing tightly like a
scar over the site of so many scalpels,
the loss of so many shoes.
The absence of feeling.
The feeling of being me, when I am so
few other things too.

This is the hand. Talking.

This is me. Not talking
to the one who exists at the still centre of the storm.
The one I have never seen. Only smelt.
The smell of lost flowers.
The smell of lost hair.
Eyes that opened once, flashed
like water under the sun,
spontaneously, and then were gone.
Beneath the black rock of fear.

This is me. Talking.

I cannot do anything else.
Cannot run, jump, climb, skip,
hurry, walk to the end of the sky.
Barely stand without falling over.
Because it is only the hand that
holds me up, that holds me onto
the narrow path, where there are no handholds,
only deep and empty falling.

But the hand is mortal.

It is not God.

It must burn.

Is anyone listening?

The Foot

The foot is a hole.
A stone.
A black stone.
A hole made by the stone
before the hole was made.
A hole that the stone cannot get out of,
no matter how black, and blacker still,
its skin goes –
Until its skin begins to crack, and
pieces flake off.
Chunks of rock falling into
the black hole that the foot grows
beneath its shadow.

The foot is a stone.
Underneath the stone is a hole
that stretches and shrinks and
stretches again as the wind blows.

The hole smells like words left a long time
in the crevice between two teeth.
Like words that have been closed up
too long in the dark pit of the mouth.
Sweating all night. And sleepless
in the day.

The foot is a hole made by a shard
of memory.
It walked through black mud
one morning on the edge of a brown lake,
where the birds waded deep up to their cries,
up to their blue wings.
It walked through the black mud and
into the lake.
And the water was not cold,
the foot said.
Come in, the foot said. The water is warm.

Look.
And it bent and scooped up the old skin
from the surface of the lake and
flung it up into the air.

And the flakes of water flew.

And the flakes of water fell.
And the foot came up out of the water
and it was red.
It was red where the flakes of water
had fallen upon it and cut it –
called out to it its new name.

Its new name was loss.
And rot.

The foot remembers the brown lake
always, and longs to return
to the warm water, to the impenetrable depths,
lurking with the voices of fishes.

It remembers the brown lake
with its long waving hair and its green eyes,
and it wants to laugh again, loudly,
the way the long grass does.
It wants to laugh again.
But there is a hole.
There is the hole made by the red stone
that does not heal.
The hole that never closes over.
Even when it seems to.

I hold the foot in my hand every night,
spit onto it.
I spit into its red hole and
mix the spit with sand and honey,
and pack it full. I pack the hole full
every night, and when I go to sleep

I dream that the hole is growing a skin over it.
That a wide bridge is falling out of the sky,
and that it lands on the foot,
and covers the deep distance
between the edges of the red hole.

The foot pretends that it has something to say.
That the fishes in the brown lake and
the birds in the air and the stones, too,
in the black desert
want to hear what it has to say.

But to be honest,
it has all been said before.

The Foot (the other one)

The other foot is stupid.

And small.

And not worth talking about.

The Shoulder

Fire most times.
And ice the others.
Fire when the ice has melted,
and standing is impossible.

Fire when the wind blows the night over,
when the invisible river running through the night
runs out of breath.

Fire most times.

And others a blade
like a butcher's,
a hammer, a chisel: bone and tissue
separating every day and returning
with every step.

The Foot Re-visited

The other foot is second in line.

It is not the cause, but the effect.

It is not the action,
but the echo that remains and waits
long after the air has returned
to stillness.

The other foot is a fish
without a backbone.
It is a pale creature from the bottom of the sea.
A desire without a shell.
Eyeless and slow.

It hears everything around it –
the whisperings and the giggles, the loud staring and
the soft pity of the eyes.
It hears everything,
but cannot see any of it.
It knows that the bottom of the sea
is not the same as the surface,
that the darkness is not the same as sunlight.
But it is unable to choose.
Its choice was already made.
Long before the land struggled out of the water.

It can only respond.

It is a response.

But (oh!)
how it longs to be the action.

The Wrist

The wrist, the right one,
is a wrench.

The wrist, not the left, is rust.

It is red metal amongst stone.
It is brittle tin. It is clanking iron.

The wrist is unsettled.
It does not join or turn or fold or meet.

It grinds, stone against stone, midday
sunlight against old iron.
Cold night against cold stars.

It is a sharp moon. A blunt moon.
Made blunt on the blade of a hill.

The wrist, my wrist, my right,
is all that holds me up.

Keeps me perpendicular
to the black grave.

AFTERWARDS

a tree without light

a sky with no bones

and a wind that rises and falls.

a book without eyes

a chair with no legs

and a window that opens and shuts.

a hand without feeling

a foot with no nerves

and a mouth that swallows and spits.

***

he was always whispering

there was a draft in his mouth.

he was always tramping

there was blood and water in his boots.

and when he sat down to empty his hand

he found himself filling it instead.

***

then it began to slow down

the motor of the sky.

and suddenly it seemed to him

as if standing still   and not standing

were one and the same thing.

as if opening   and closing

happened all at once   in the same

place   at the same time.

***

he drove with the sun directly in his eyes

the city was setting

the haze of the day was impenetrable

and the hills were without light

they made a noose around the city

the road was long

and the long road lengthened before him

and he thought that he would close his eyes

for a second

and then open them again

and it would be as if he were refreshed

it would be as if he had been asleep

beneath long water where the road no longer moaned

it would be as if he had closed his eyes

and a light had appeared on the inside

so he folded away his arms

with his hands at the end of them

and a rusty hinge at the beginning

and he covered the sun with his tongue

there was no sound inside him

nothing moved in his head anymore

and then it happened

suddenly all of the sky was behind him

the haze cleared instantly

he could move freely for the first time in his life

without holding on to a thing.

* * *

there is a cold in the white neck

and the exposed wrists burn

the doves and the weavers and the old tractor moan

the workman is piling up wood behind the rusted shed

the hillside is silent   with pale thin grass

the trees too   flat and bare and black

and the dry leaves rustle   like tracing paper

and a crowned crane crosses slowly across the sky

low sky   lowered like a rope by one unseen from an attic

and the thought returns   the same one   never different

the thought that if it were all to stop

now   the whole of every thing   then

then it would not have been said   that thing

that terrible thing that would have made it all worthwhile

that thing which   because it was unknown

unknown because it was unsaid   would therefore

never be known

by the white wrists

by the exposed neck.

* * *

and into the next day he goes

like a blind dog

sniffing everything

trusting his empty blue eyes

to always know

where his feet should go.

* * *

and then it is the moment

when he must close his arm   like a pocket knife

and accept that he will never be able to sever his link

with himself   that even when he should die

it would not be anyone else's death

except his own.

Acknowledgements

Some of these poems were published, in different versions, in: *Carapace*, *New Contrast*, *Botsotso*, *New Coin*, *Green Dragon*, *Timbila*, *Fidelities*, *Inglis House Poetry*, *A Hudson View*, *Flash Magazine*, *Southern Rain Poetry*, *LitNet*, *African-Writing* and *Disability Studies Quarterly*.

The poems 'Boy', 'Three Trees' and 'Anatomy' were written during a collaborative residency at the Caversham Centre for Writers and Artists, Lidgetton, 2008.

The poem 'Opening' was written at Solitude Retreat Centre, Petrus Stroom, 2007.

'Anatomy' received the DALRO award for the best poem published in *New Coin* magazine in 2008.

'Boy' was nominated for the 2010 Pushcart prize.

Special thanks to Robert Berold for his incisive comments and support. And to Joan Metelerkamp and Mindy Stanford for their important suggestions.

Production costs for this book were made possible by a research grant from the University of KwaZulu-Natal, under the auspices of the National Research Foundation.